Y0-DJN-525

What to do
when your mom or dad says...
"TURN OFF
THE WATER AND LIGHTS!"

By
JOY WILT BERRY

Living Skills Press
Fallbrook, California

Copyright ©1984 Joy Wilt Berry
All rights reserved.
Printed in the United States of America.
Library of Congress Catalog Card Number: 83-080844
ISBN 0-941510-23-9

Dear Parents,

"TURN OFF THE WATER AND LIGHTS!" How often have you reminded your children to do this? Have you ever wondered why children do not remember to turn the water and lights off on their own? We often assume that children will want to cooperate with our requests even when they don't understand *why* they should turn off the water and lights, turn down the heat, or close the refrigrator door. Children need to know *why* and *how* they can help to save energy in their homes.

Energy conservation is a household responsibility. It requires each member of the family to do his or her share to eliminate energy and water waste in the home. When children understand that they have important responsibilities within the family, they are more willing to learn what is necessary to carry out those responsibilities.

TURN OFF THE WATER AND LIGHTS will explain to your children the whys and hows of energy conservation. With this book, you can help your children to save water and energy by—

1. Explaining the need for conservation in your home because of:—
   • dwindling energy resources and water supplies, and
   • the high cost of home energy use.
2. Demonstrating exactly what children can do to help save energy.
3. Delegating energy-saving responsibilities appropriate to your children's ages.
4. Setting an example by assuming adult responsibilities for energy conservation. (Installing insulation, weather stripping, special light fixtures, and shower heads are important tasks beyond the energy-saving responsibilities of a child.)
5. Including your children in your energy conservation efforts

and sharing the results with them whenever possible. Recycling aluminum cans is a good example of a family project that results in—
- shared activity
- energy saved
- money saved
- money earned

Each of our homes is a unique environment of energy consumers. You can demonstrate to your children how the energy-conservation hints in this book can best be applied to your own home. Setting an example of home energy conservation is one of the most effective ways for you to encourage those habits in your children.

The energy crunch is here to stay. Our children must learn to live productively in a world of diminishing resources where there no longer is any room for waste. **TURN OFF THE WATER AND LIGHTS** will introduce your children to energy conservation as a lifelong commitment.

Sincerely,

Joy Wilt Berry

Has your mother or father ever told you to . . .

Whenever you are told to turn off the water and lights, do you wonder. . .

If any of this sounds familiar to you, you are going to **love** this book.

Because it will explain why your parents want you to turn off the water and lights and will tell you how to respond to their request.

Human beings need water and energy in order to survive and grow. Water and energy come from natural resources found in and around the earth.

The earth has a limited supply of these natural resources. If they are used up, there will be no more water or energy for human beings to use.

For this reason, it is important not to waste natural resources. This means not wasting the water or the energy the natural resources create.

It is also important to do all we can to put the natural resources back into the earth.

When your parents ask you to turn off the water and lights, they are asking you to do something that will save the earth's natural resources. When you do what they have asked you to do, you are contributing to your own survival and growth as well as to that of other human beings.

Turning the earth's natural resources into usable water and energy takes a great deal of work. Factories, workers, and machines are needed to do this work, and money is needed to pay for it.

For this reason, your parents must pay for the water and energy you use. The more you use, the more money your parents have to pay.

When your parents ask you to turn off the water and lights, they are asking you to do something that will save money. The money you help save can be used for other things that your family may need or want.

There are many things you can do besides turning off water and lights to help preserve the earth's natural resources and to help save money. You will find them in the rest of this book.

SAVING RESOURCES INDOORS

Water

Water should not be wasted. Therefore, it should not flow from a faucet without being used.

- At the sink, do not allow the water to run while you are brushing your teeth. Instead, wet your toothbrush, then turn the water off until you are ready to rinse your mouth.
- In the shower, turn the water off when you soap your body and shampoo your hair. Turn it on again to rinse yourself off.

If you need to run tap water to get hot water—

• use the cool water to run the garbage disposal, or
• put the cool water in a pitcher, refrigerate it, and
  use it for drinking water.

If you need to run shower water to get hot water,
catch the cold water in a container and—

• use it to water plants, or
• put it in the washing machine to use for the next
  wash load.

- Make sure that the water faucet is turned completely off after you are finished using it. Do not leave it dripping.

- If you notice a leaky faucet, report it to your parents so that they can have it repaired.

Do not use more water than you actually need.

- Do not fill the bathtub full. If you fill the tub half-full, you will have more than enough water to take a bath.

- Use the toilet to dispose of body wastes only and do not flush it unless it is necessary. It is more economical, for instance, to throw a soiled facial tissue in a wastebasket than to flush it down the toilet.

- The temperature gauge on the water heater should be set at approximately 140°F. or lower. This will save energy and prevent rusting.

- A cover for the water heater is an economical way to keep the water hot.

- Use the cold-water faucet when you need small amounts of water. In this way, the hot-water heater will not be turned on automatically when it is not necessary.

Lights

A light should be turned on only when it is needed. It is wasteful to have lights on in rooms that are not being used.

- You should turn out the light in a room with regular (incandescent) light if you plan to be out of the room for more than 3 minutes at a time.
- You should turn out the light in a room with fluorescent light if you plan to be out of the room for more than 15 minutes at a time.

Turning a light on and off too much will shorten the life of the bulb.

- In a room with regular (incandescent) light, the light should be left on when you leave the room for 3 minutes or less.
- In a room with fluorescent light, the light should be left on when you leave the room for 15 minutes or less.

Heat and Cold

It is important not to allow yourself to get too hot or too cold. For your comfort and safety, you will need to keep the temperature in your house at approximately 68°F. in the winter and 78°F. in the summer.

It takes a lot of energy to run a furnace or air conditioner. Therefore, you should not depend on these things alone to maintain the appropriate temperature in your house. There are other energy-saving things that you can do to keep your house warm in the winter and cool in the summer.

Make sure that all the openings are closed when you are heating or cooling your house. This will keep the heat or cool air from escaping.

- Keep the doors and windows closed.
- Close the damper when the fireplace is not in use.

It is also a good idea to keep the drapes and shades closed on hot or cold days. This will reduce heat loss or gain through the windows.

If the temperature is 68°F. and you still feel
cold—

- wear warmer clothes, or put on a sweater or
  jacket, or
- increase your body movements so that you will
  generate body heat.

If the temperature is 78°F. and you still feel hot—

- wear lighter-weight clothing,
- lower your body heat by decreasing your body movements,
- sponge your body off with a damp, cool cloth, or
- put a damp, cool cloth on your forehead or on the back of your neck.

During the night, when the weather is cold—

- Keep warm by using extra bedding.

During the night, when the weather is hot—

- Turn the air conditioner off and open the windows. Keep cool by using less bedding and by wearing lightweight bedclothes.
- You can also save energy by turning off the air conditioner one-half hour before you leave home.

Appliances

It takes energy to run an appliance. Thus, the less you use an appliance, the less energy you will use. If you can do a task without an appliance, do it. For example—

- Wash and dry the dishes instead of using a dishwasher.
- Wash a small load of clothes by hand rather than using a washing machine.
- Hang clothes up to dry rather than using a clothes dryer.
- Dry your hair with a towel rather than using a hair dryer.

Do not leave appliances running when they are not being used. For example—

- Do not leave the TV on if it is not being watched.
- Do not leave a radio on if no one is listening to it.
- Do not leave a record or tape player on when it has finished playing the recording or tape.
- Do not leave curling irons, steam curlers, or electric irons plugged in when no one is using them.

27

If you have a choice, use smaller appliances whenever possible as larger appliances use more energy.

Because most people and businesses use their large appliances during the day, the energy supply is limited at this time. Thus, you should use large appliances early in the morning or late at night whenever possible.

Using the Washing Machine

You save water and energy by doing the following—

- Wash a full load each time you use the washing machine. Adjust the water level of the machine to accommodate the size of the wash load. Be sure to use as little water as necessary.
- Use the short cycle on the washing machine whenever possible.

Using the Dryer

You save energy in the following way—

- Do not use the dryer to dry just one or two articles of clothing. Hang them up to dry, instead.
- Do not overload the dryer as it will take longer for the clothes to dry.
- Turn the dryer off when the clothes are dry. Do not allow the dryer to run unnecessarily.
- Clean the lint from the screen each time you use the dryer as it takes longer for clothes to dry when the lint screen is full.

Using the Refrigerator and Freezer

When the refrigerator or freezer door is left open, the cold air escapes and energy is needed to replace it. Thus, it is important to remember the following—

- If possible, decide what you are going to get before you open the refrigerator door.
- Open and close the door as quickly as possible.
- Make sure the door is not left ajar when you close it.

Using the Stove and Oven

- Small pans heated on large burners waste energy. Thus, you should match the bottom of the pan to the size of the burner.
- Do not waste energy by using the oven to heat a single item. Instead, wait until there are several things to heat and then heat all of them in the oven at the same time.

Using the Dishwasher

You save water and energy in the following way—

- Wash a full load each time you use the dishwasher.
- Use the short cycle of the dishwasher whenever possible.
- Turn the dishwasher off after the last rinse cycle. Open the door slightly and allow the air to dry the dishes.

When You Leave Home for Several Days

- Pull the plugs on the television set(s) and all small appliances.
- Turn off the air conditioner.
- Remind your parents to turn down the thermostats on the water heater, refrigerator, and freezer.
- Turn off washing-machine faucets.

SAVING RESOURCES OUTDOORS
Water

Do not leave running water unattended. Turn it off immediately after it has served its purpose. For example—

- When watering the garden or lawn, turn the water on, wait to see that the plants have received enough water, then turn the water off.
- If you cannot wait while the water is running, set a time limit for the watering and return to turn the water off when the time is up.

- When you water a garden or lawn during the heat of the day, much of the water is lost through evaporation. Thus, it is best to water in the early morning or in the evening.
- Because weeds take water, too, eliminate them from your lawn and garden.

- If you want to play in the water from the hose or the sprinkler, play in an area that needs water so that the water will not be wasted.

Use a broom, not a hose, to clean driveways,
sidewalks, and steps.

Automobiles

When you wash a car, save water by using a bucket of water rather than a hose. The hose should be used only to rinse the car off.

Gasoline should not be wasted. Therefore, use a car for transportation only when it is necessary. Whenever possible—

- walk,
- ride a bike,
- use public transportation, such as buses or trains, or
- share rides with your friends.

Whenever possible, avoid using the car air conditioner. When the weather is hot, wear lightweight clothing and leave the windows rolled down.

OTHER WAYS TO SAVE RESOURCES

Recycling

One way to save energy is to use items for as long as possible. Therefore, you should remember to do the following—

- Take care of an item when you use it, and store it carefully when finished.
- Repair items that are worn or broken.

Other Recycling Ideas

Items that are not being used should be given to people who will use them. For example—

- Unused metal hangers should be returned to the dry cleaner.
- Outgrown clothes should be given to someone who can use them.

Items should be used as completely as possible. For example—

- An entire sheet of paper (including both sides) should be used.
- Used plastic items should be cleaned and reused whenever possible.
- Used containers should be reused whenever possible.

Old things (such as paper, bottles, or cans) should be returned to recycling centers so they can be made into new things.

New things should be made out of old things. For example:

- Produce gardens can be grown from seeds, roots, or cuttings.
- Compost (a kind of fertilizer) can be made out of dead grass, leaves, garbage, and animal waste.

Disposables

Disposables are items that are to be used one time and then thrown away. These items are created to earn a profit from people's desire for convenience. Disposables are convenient, but they don't really disappear. They eventually are burned in incinerators, which use up energy and contribute to air pollution, or they are buried in garbage dumps and landfills, which contribute to land pollution.

For this reason, you should avoid using disposables whenever possible. For example, use cloth towels rather than paper towels, or use plates that can be washed rather than paper plates.

If you must use a disposable item, use it sparingly. For example, don't waste toilet paper and use as little facial tissue as possible.

There are three ways to conserve energy when you buy products:

1. Buy things that last a long time.
2. Buy beverages in returnable containers.
3. Whenever possible, buy recycled paper products. It takes less energy to make recycled paper than it does to make paper from trees. Also, by using recycled paper products, you are conserving our trees—one of our most beautiful natural resources.

THE END of wasting water and energy!